LISTEN

BEFORE

TRANSMIT

OTHER BOOKS BY DANI COUTURE

POETRY
Good Meat
Sweet
Yaw

FICTION
Algoma

LISTEN BEFORE TRANSMIT

DANI COUTURE

A Buckrider Book

© Dani Couture, 2018

No part of this publication may be reproduced, stored in a retrieval system or transmitted, in any form or by any means, without the prior written consent of the publisher or a license from the Canadian Copyright Licensing Agency (Access Copyright). For an Access Copyright license, visit www.accesscopyright.ca or call toll free to 1-800-893-5777.

Buckrider Books is an imprint of Wolsak and Wynn Publishers.

Cover and interior design: Natalie Olsen, Kisscut Design
Cover image: Dani Couture
Author photograph: Roberta Baker
Typeset in Novel Pro
Printed by Coach House Printing Company Toronto, Canada

The publisher gratefully acknowledges the support of the Canada Council for the Arts, the Ontario Arts Council and the Government of Canada.

Buckrider Books
280 James Street North
Hamilton, Ontario
Canada L8R 2L3

Library and Archives Canada Cataloguing in Publication
Couture, Dani, 1978–, author
Listen before transmit / Dani Couture.
Poems.
ISBN 978-1-928088-54-7 (softcover)
1. Title.
PS8605.O92L57 2018   C811'.6   C2018-900523-8

I.M. JOS. COUTURE

(1929–2015)

We are always halfway there
when we are here.

FANNY HOWE
"By Halves"

CONTENTS

I COME AROUND WITH APPETITE TO PARTIES I
YOU WORE OUT YOUR WELCOME WITH RADIANT ABILITY 3
PROTOTYPE 5
LISTEN BEFORE TRANSMIT 6
MOTHER, ORDER OCTOPODA 7
PIONEER 14 8
SMALL ORANGE AND BLUE 10
REPORT ON THE BRIGHT SPOTS ON CERES 11
WATCHED BY THE DRONE 13
THE OMEGA TRICK 14
FORECAST 15
MEMOIR 16

BLACK SEA NETTLE 21
A BRIEF HISTORY 23
CLONAL 26
OR IN ARGUMENT 28
MINUS TIME 29
A CASUAL DEFENCE 30
REPORT ON THE STATUS OF RACCOONS ON FERN AVENUE 32
SLEEP STUDY 33
RED-EYE 34
ALMANAC 35
SQUALL 36
FLYBY 38

WHAT HE ATE DID NOT SO MUCH RELIEVE HIS HUNGER 43
ARC 45
VIRGA 46
SYMPATHETIC STRINGS 48
THIS IS GRAVITY 49
MOTHER, ORDER APPLE 50
FINAL REPORT ON THE STATUS OF RACCOONS ON FERN AVENUE 51
ANOTHER EARTH 53
MOTE 55
SHIFT OF OCCUPANT 56
PARALLAX 58
LAST DAYS 60
CONTACT 62
TRANSIT OF MERCURY 63

I COME AROUND WITH APPETITE TO PARTIES

An evening carousel of who died, which
winds ribboned down, and the difference
between something bruised or broken.

The treatment is the same. No, it's not
enough to say you were there, felt it snap,
or shuttered a photo. Instead, run a man's

finger along your chest and ask, *See?*
Feel that. Right there? I think it's broken.
Pain, like living, requires corroboration.

So he palms your left breast and pushes
until it gives. A sound. His opinion.
A hole dug and the declaration

of empty space as something new.
An inverse peak. He confirms what's already
inside you. Rib dispossessed of its hold,

the punchline out of sync. Meanwhile,
a mine shaft in South America collapses.
A deflation, though you are filling with things

that are not yours. What's broken rises
like loaves. You've been researching
these injuries, this news, for hours.

Tell me I'm right. That there's a difference
between a spout and funnel. A fracture
and separation. A plane that was cleared to fly

or wasn't. If the Buk was stolen or given.
Birds kettle and people are kettled.
The kettle I forgot sings a high whistle.

The dead remain dead except we keep
finding new uses for them. A quartz
of quail's breast perched on worn gauntlet

can satisfy multiple interests.
How light the claw that only takes
What's offered when offered. We're told

every day is a rehearsal. Set the action.
Reach your end point. Reset. Remember
to look up and to the left. You're running

for your life. *The effects will be added
later, but we need your fear now.*
They gave me a blue and white dress,

sewed me in, but said I could keep
my own black shoes. Said, *If need be,
we'll cut you out at the end.*

YOU WORE OUT YOUR WELCOME
WITH RADIANT ABILITY

Tarred, tarried July above the finger-point
of bylaw. Quiet men

are quietly roofing in runic arrests.
Progress can be stopped

with minor internal damage and a length of rope
short enough to miss the point.

Everything can and will happen at once.

Except the sun's light, which is not full,
but an incomplete weave that covers the most
controversial areas of interest.

In a cab, you know without lesson it's better to talk
to your hours-dead cat wedged into its carrier
like an overstuffed closet of furs.

It's okay. Hello, Little One. Hello.

It's better for everyone
if you decide it's better for everyone.
There is the take-away. In coolers,

the dead become firmer in their resolve
to remain firm. At home, celery softens and pools
in the corner you regularly remember to forget.

Telephones channel the regrets of future days.
Drift through

intersections like a planchette you're directing
but would deny. The roads are being torn up
for new roads. Anyone could have
predicted that, even you.

Heat gullies best intentions
and hours lean. Work crews
adopt fresh pace. You will find out
the work you do is internal. You will
undo it. A spill of vinegar into the milk.

You are being closed into the hour
like an exhibit. When the glass comes down
a voice will say, It's okay, it's okay.

Air conditioners drone in precision flocks.
The air will last until it doesn't.

PROTOTYPE

Whenever a shadow crawls past, we look up. A million years of instinct, the oldest unrequited love story retold with a crouch. This fear a helical hand-me-down – improvised tool for a machine no longer in use. Or an alloy egg waiting to crack and become the winged thing that flies overhead. In Saint-Cloud, the holy measure is measured against itself and found wanting. Its sisters ripple out in cloth and watt while our milk is kept in museums. Here on Earth everything stands for one thing, or what it used to be. Atomic placeholders. When someone dies, we can say they were reorganized – moon rock to presidential paperweight, or moon rock lost among earth rocks, or moon rock catalogued and forgotten in equally forgotten cupboard. Over time, inevitably, substitutions are offered. Changeling economies of spec. There are hours that come with a price for having seen them. Nightly, the moon cues a dimly projected morning. Shut your eyes and hold out your hands. Wait for the night deposit of your picul, which is not mine. Tell me, how did you keep splitting only to become one thing?

LISTEN BEFORE TRANSMIT

After Peter Gizzi

The connection severs itself due to

your finger hovers A pause

inactivity of a predetermined kind

exhalation of the hesitation that

More so to know what

their patterns Confute yourself

who can identify what's missing

room unknown to him alone

Buried in you like a tumour for

What we call *the good kind*

Instructions were mixed Handled

Who thinks back will end

Losing is in the looking or

I think I said goodbye

The dial radiates options

it always did It always

MOTHER, ORDER OCTOPODA

What the prosthetist offers is no loose banister dowel,
cane relaxed of its smirk or even hockey stick
with its single, clubbed foot. *Once, in a lab, an octopus*
reached out of its tank to pet a cat. He casts
a water glass half-empty for your half-full. A plastic vase
for your single, stumped stem. At home, you crab
across the kitchen on borrowed limb until
you taste iron, some spidering alloy that's weaved
itself through the meat of you. Socked away
what did you secret to the incinerator, bury
in slim drift of departing marrow? *I could never*
eat something that was empathetic. In a dream,
your missing leg repeated and stacked – a cord
of winter wood. The chance to rise ahead of yourself
as ash. *So many things I've touched are dead,*
I'm beginning to take it personally. Nights
when you try to massage the void, do you feel
the tether – slim, neural kite string that ties not
to the bolt of lost ankle, but transmission failure?
The excess of the cephalopod. Sweet tentacle bloom.
Once, in a recovery room, I reached to touch
your damp crown, counted what remained: three
hearts, one hooked beak, the steep slope of empty
space beneath tidal sheets. *It could do with less.*

PIONEER 14

Addendum to the pudendal cleft rubbed
off, out, or plaqued shut with gold. Our god,
one of them, magic-tricked a woman
from bone.

> We call this humour.

As part of a codicil, should vandals – interstellar
dust or cosmic key – scratch a fissure, a separate and distant
recording will play.

> A cosmic Easter egg.

A bartender in Wilmington who remarked
salsa dancers make the best guests. Impossible
to tell if there are twenty or ten in the room
once attached. It has been said we are best
and worst when organized.

Jet propulsion will eventually erupt
and cause a break between her legs,
at which point she will take off.

The man's ninth finger, his cardinal
rose, will orient you to Earth.

His breasts are lacking, but don't point it out.
We call them *pecs.* His nipples are seeds
birds feed on. We have birds. *Do you?*

> *Are you?*

The woman has nipples, too, which
are shown, but may not be in future.
We are creatures capable

of compromise. The male's globular
organs, half-buried in his face,
are decorative stones. The woman's, holes.
Others are missing entirely, etched
onto other plaques. Look for future

crafts to explain flora. We've shot fauna
up, but brought them back.
Understand our sentimentality. Our nature
we call human. Other times, humane.

At the top of the plate, the hyperfine
transition of hydrogen. Two clefts
that bleed roughly twelve times
a year until they become stateless.

       All that we know

is expressed by the angle of the woman's
hip, cocked. The ball of her bare foot.

       Please,

when you come, call us
Linda. And we will kiss our own
open palm and call you *ours*.

SMALL ORANGE AND BLUE

A white T-shirt
with small orange and blue
horses galloping
uniformly in rows.
Trample along, invert
nipples, tumble into
the single umbilical
knot. Break legs.
Require a degree
of compassion
compassion will not
allow. So neigh
and everyone
stays awake.
Tomorrow, no
bother with simple
armour against
imagined elements,
or curtsying sleep
in with formality.
The dressage of clouds
of white moths
stickered to bare
windows, pressing
their fur-trimmed bodies
against every light
I've left turned on
in the absence of anyone
who might turn
them off. Whoever
said a lighthouse
wasn't an invitation?

REPORT ON THE BRIGHT SPOTS ON CERES

We're speculating on our speculations.
    Bright spots. Plumes of ice? We'll know

once we draw in closer. Our Cyclops Dawn.
    There's rumour that within months, Ceres's

status will change. A Houston girl who turns
    sixteen. The debut of ninety-nine cents

become a single dollar. Come official word,
    a thousand children will be primed to string

floss and foam additions to the world's solar
    system mobiles. They'll learn it's okay

to admit others were wrong. And will
    be wrong again. We're still smarting over Pluto.

Our internal mnemonics refuse alteration. How
    many times do I have to tell you

you never stop loving someone. In Switzerland,
    versions of us are smashing microscopic

holes into the known universe with the idea
    that they, like us, will radiate

and die in short time. I sent them a letter
    to say the platypus has poisonous spurs

and the huntsman spider is mostly harmless.
    I've done my part. Come Friday, look

to see if the lights go out or burn brighter. For now,
    textbook pages tremble as each letter dilates

to accommodate what we hope for against
    what we need to hope for. The mechanical failure

of our best pitch set forth on a slow drift.
    We've breached the hearth

of the original view. What was it I needed to do?
    I can't recall what it was I once thought.

WATCHED BY THE DRONE

The delicate piece of technology cost hundreds
          of thousands of dollars.
Better than human.
I think it is a biological imperative.
So hysterical.
Apologies for not using the proper scientific term.
Humour me.
I am watching a legal webinar on position paper
          writing that I paid for.
Welcome to my world.
Do we all just live in your mind, godhead?

How is your heart?
It's diagnostic, not something that happened
          to you on the street.
Were you in a fugue state when you did it?
Didn't he even wonder where she was building the bridges?
          Did he ask to see them?
And no I am not joking.
The build was most satisfying.

What the fuck is that art behind you?
I'd never won a door prize in my life.
I've been monitoring my facial expression over the day
          in relation to headaches. This is me looking
          at tax forms online.
Now I can just give them a large canyon
          in a new dimension.
          Easy.
Yes, I am the public. You hadn't figured that out yet?
          This whole city is full of empty houses but mine.
Her wealth was an ill-concealed open secret. We knew it
          when she pulled the billfold from her purse
          on the streetcar and started counting.
Is it possible you are not human?
I am famished.

THE OMEGA TRICK

I want this to be the last thing I'll ever do,
to stop here and say I'll go no further.
KATE HALL
"Overnight a Horse Appeared"

A portside slap of white hieroglyph warns objects are larger
than they appear and do not disappear beneath the surface.
As if something that would dare that close would turn back.

This intent has legs. Too late, I've already forgotten
I can die. But if I did, it would be some signature trick:
a released fish knuckleballed into the lake and taken up
in flight. This desire to get close is all opposing mirrors –
the universe trying to both see and collapse into itself.

Some days, there exists two types of hunger,
except, in the end, only one. The first eats the other.

It's how I imagine these galaxies we're told to believe in
when I've never even been to California.

Upriver, a parade through a stalled parade of empty
buildings. Huge, clumsy machinations Oz'd with Model T
descendants. The waters no longer run red or court fire.
We've found better blends to run off. Crushed pills
in spoonfuls of corn syrup. Come, the algae blooms
are so thick, we can walk on water we can't drink.

At a certain hour, the sky and river look twinned,
an untilled grey, and I can understand how a plane can be
piloted into water thinking it was the right way up.

14

FORECAST

After a winter pipe burst, pulped all I'd kept, but if asked,
could not recall, I became the sort who carried talismans
from countries I did not belong to. The possibilities
of when a saviour might appear if you knew how
to summon her mistranslated in the handoff. How *gift* in Danish
can mean both *poison* and *marriage*. In time, I improvised
my own luck. When a ceramic horse – a gift – broke,
I kept the largest pieces arranged inside a cracked curio.
Consulted the remaining leg on matters of finance.
A section of mane on health. A shell of belly I kept tucked
in the cup of my bra. Predicted that over time
the sharp edges would buff smooth against my skin
like a chipped tooth tossed to sea and did.
In turn, the horse asked after weather, wheat futures, tides
of lotto numbers, what good thing will go bad
and what bad will turn good. To which I told each piece
a different outcome. Watched its parts pulse then polarize.
There came a point when the mare ground herself finely
into dust, laid silent and left me lonely. Later,
in a grocery store, I stood under the bald fluorescent suns,
stationed myself at the centre of the abundance, made a wish
on the jagged Morse of the sensor doors, quietly asked
the world for more and then, if it was listening, just a little more.

MEMOIR

The bronze statue of a soldier sits astride
a bronze horse imagined exactly 1.5 times

larger than any known breed. A slayed dragon,
artfully reclined in death, tops well-chiselled notes

on an empire. If the enemy is imagined
as a dragon, the enemy will be unaware

we know they are our enemy. Or recall they
once were and may be again. The recurring

apogee of goals and timelines. In the park, hostas
proliferate, stab up in spring like strip spikes

that puncture all to arrest one. Like dreaming once
to end all waking. Melatonin jet lag, sleep, and here

you are able to float and horses ride men above
a conflict of dented texts. Small details, contrails,

threaded through to make it almost believable – a lie
from the one in your bed, but from and to yourself.

Recombinant data. At rest, your brain selects
a Zeppelin to tour a city of spires. Math

was never your strong suit. You were told
to bring three adapters. The pleasure of plugging in

everything at once is undeniable. By percentage,
the galleries had more heads than bodies.

Outside of one, a man, granite, holds up the head
of a woman, granite, emancipated from her body.

Saving her, punishing her, or both. You failed to read
the plaque. A second gallery welcomes visitors

with bay window–sized breasts fashioned in three
colours of neon piping, which, in your mind, flash

OPEN, OPEN, OPEN. Artist's intent aside, you enter
the gallery like a fisherman's knot and leave hooked.

This where you felt most at home away from home.
Home where the grackles are the size of ravens,

ravens the size of dogs, dogs the size of horses,
yet women still variable according to need and purpose.

At the departure gate, you ask a guard if you speak
a different language than your father, are you ensured security

of your own thought outside his borders? Everyone said
this was a long way to go to be somewhere else.

BLACK SEA NETTLE

If the relationship to one's body is expressed
algebraically, let every variable be a decorative
tuber. A golden mean of worry buried
by one animal and dug up by a double.

What's tucked up or down and not talking?
Consider the colour, the space of days
between what we know to be good, other,
or another and decide. The story of a person

who cut their foot and died within five hours.
They were pregnant, or had a tumour. It was
a black spot on their left shin after having
mown the lawn. During an eclipse,

they looked at the sun without their
daughter's pinhole camera. A neighbour
who hadn't washed their hands
after breaking eggs for bread pudding.

Eighty-five, unmarried, no children.
Mail snowed the summer door until
they were discovered. They were never born.
It was their fault. It won't happen

again. During a date, one offers to the other
that they exist in a medical textbook
in England. Parts collapsed early.
A bottle in, they invite you

to feel how their small bones are fused
like mercury. This is a fairy tale, where
the woodsman's axe draws the wrong blood.
Except the woodsman is you. Is also them.

Sheet stain and the indifferent shrug
of something you can do without,
but are you sure? You've made a blood
oath with so many things some days

your body begs to follow. From the inside
out, jellyfish, the soft slip of fingers, tentacle
reversal. A confusing of predatory intent.
Once, teenaged, in the back of a red Renault

in Chrysler country, the driver stared
into the flat tooth of his rear-view mirror
and said, I don't trust anything
that bleeds for five days and doesn't die.

A BRIEF HISTORY

De proche en proche, votre science mettra notre espèce à l'abri.
J-H ROSNY AÎNÉ (JOSEPH HENRI HONORÉ BOEX)
Les Navigateurs de l'infini

Witness to a swarm of false jellies that alternate
between yellow

smiley face *Thank Yous* and black *Come Agains.*
Moulds'

positives released to their new wild gyre.
Inland, a roughed-up stuffed

animal forgotten in '83 Pizza Hut now as buried
as any body

even if the weather has been digging up graves.
Eras cycle,

float down washed-out highways. A soft
lashing

against your leg says you have lost
an understanding

of your surroundings and cannot go back.
What feels like

a small death is only a tolling carillon's
passing attention.

A blister. A moment in the key of minor. The index
of our refraction

is negligible but enough for you to believe
we're still evolving

or able to change even basic habits. Forgetting to
lock the front door,

or learning to forget. Our life cycles
are hardly understood

in comparison to x – the variable we have
not yet discovered

but expect to listen to Chuck Berry.
We're growing

through one another like finger traps
and will soon

turn two hundred with minimal consequence.
Still, recalcitrant

Earth may one day buck us toward
the closest passable exo.

No matter, we're heavy, require launching,
are many.

We have our time, if not the time
of others. Tonight,

we remain here, waterlogged with cured
nostalgia.

Our memories revealed by salt and suspended
in gelatin.

Some improvised, analog, carved into gold fired
at some future target.

Sit with me. The math of tonight's half light,
heaven's melted

plastics, renders us moderately more attractive,
which, in part,

keeps us breeding to extend the thoughts
we've been thinking.

To date, I've come to understand
humans

like photos of themselves, like their pasts
– taken

at a distance. At a midpoint
and mistakable.

Allowing one to consider that it could have
gone a different way.

And possibly did or will. You waking up
instead

of waking down to the next forty years,
which is now

the past forty years. It's been so long
since we visited

the moon, every archival photo looks taken
from a single road trip

we based our entire lives on.
Yesterday,

I purchased a second-hand tin of old
photographs

and tried to understand them as Boex's
waning Tripèdes.

But it's too late. By the time you tell someone
to look

at the harvest moon, it's reduced, gone plain
as any other night.

CLONAL

The brain, at first, some chordate
dew worm uprooted

from flooded soil. Later,
it foams a cloud

against folded horizon. White
space that's easy

on the eye, but not
the mind. It leans

like a comma against
what's closest. Its presence

or absence changing
the meaning.

My first word was
hereditary.

The second and third:
is it?

When I look at her, I am
looking at a machine

of which I am simply
a component. Not even

something that keeps her
going: toothed gear

or prehistoric swill. To look
ahead is to look her dead

on, straight, a rush of blood
at the back of the eye reflected.

A cosmic funhouse mirror.
Jimmying a car door open

with the same car's antenna.
A joyride onto the assembly line.

OR IN ARGUMENT

Birdsong so clear it sounds like foley. A dozen men
with whistles. Two, skilled, who use their mouths. Or
it's my own voice. Everything uttered out of boredom,
drunkenness, sex, or in argument, salvaged and spat back.
Unwanted and returned in parts. The overgrown roses
half-destroyed by midday buck still wearing its velvet.
Twice, I've asked the woods if anyone is there
to no response. Not even before I was born. In proximity
to a woman who painted the off-white walls off-white.
Between strokes, she wondered if I would be bad
company, which I was for years. Fingers of birch point
toward my window like schoolyard children revealing
a minor crime. The doctor who said my conception
was an impossibility, or, at least, confusing. The tumour
and I occupying the woman like deadbeat tenants
who ruin it for everyone. Who smoke the off-white yellow,
leave rot to brown the fridge. Carve up the hardwood
with our indecision and never return the keys
with thanks or the promise that everything
she hoped for, once, as a girl, was in the mail.

MINUS TIME

Who were you when you understood the sun
was simply a star? That you, in part, were made
of collapse. You, smallest sun. You're go for launch.

We could do this all night. We could do this
for a life and still end up exactly here. Who were you
when you understood the sun? How many times

have you lit the kettle's coil to leave it cold?
Tonight, feeling as uneasy as unlit neon.
You, smallest sun. You're go for launch.

A power surge brightens the light. Continuity
is constantly being restored. Who were you
when you understood the sun was simply a star?

Flip the kettle's switch to again hear the flare.
T minus the time it takes you to forget
your intention. You, smallest sun. You're go.

Walk into the backyard to see your body
radiate, irradiate every face. Who were you
when you understood the sun? You,
smallest one, you're go for launch.

A CASUAL DEFENCE

Nightly, I gather the empty in the mostly empty apartment
until it's a piece of hard, black gum to chew on
in the off-hours. From bed, a crow's scatter cache
of bobby pins into an empty water glass, windowsill,
deepest nests of hair. Casual defence against pilferage
where the front-line changes on the whim of reach
and institutional memory. Downstairs, the landlord's children
note the passing seasons with their bric-a-brac'd hallway.
The dollar store's plastic ghost with the motion sensor arm
that bends to touch my shoulder feels related.
The electric lever of passive care plasma fuels
or sometimes doesn't. *When are you coming home?*
the unmoved objects ask. They wait, and in turn are
redeployed by my own hand, parasomniacally, so as to seem,
come morning, moved by someone else. Double agenting
behind the Danish teak. Hot sauce dotting the dieffenbachia.
A conspecific who lives in the closet and never fully screws
the lid on the jam jar. Who nests blankets by the family
room radiator for a different kind of sleep. Which brings us
to the matter of the Christmas tree, its hard needles
pointing toward a new December. What started out as a joke
nobody asked to hear is now an experiment in time
travel or forestry, but I cannot decide which. I should say
I moved away so I had somewhere to return to. All of this
occasional want of family, but a refusal to put holes in
the walls. Did I tell you when I was a child I thought
I was related to Gorbachev? The Russian president's
birthmark close enough to my own beet stain
that I decoded it – a familial wink from inside
the warmth of the curved television screen? Yesterday,
my neighbour tapped a pen against his side of the wall,

so I found one and tapped back, but must have done it wrong
because he stopped. Every fall, his mice squeeze through
the cracks and shoot across my floors. They leave relaxed
atop the compost, walked out the front door. Imagine
where you could go if you didn't have a hanger
of clavicle. Your skull, a hard plug, the only obstacle.
That and your need for crumbs. Somewhere south,
researchers are placing strange dead amongst flocks
of crows, and I hope, this year, for the best.

REPORT ON THE STATUS OF RACCOONS ON FERN AVENUE

The children have elected them, en masse,
as head gardener, tastemaker, first love.
Individually, some are mistaken for escaped
house cats or nothing at all – renter's side
of a one-way mirror. Assembled, they move
as one. A giant fractal considering
the neighbourhood, licking off shingles
for the gap-toothed view of our pills,
passwords and occasional sex. Last frost
is their favourite formula. Their claws
are fashioned from pull tabs, lighter silver,
and lost earrings. The only words they know
are I *am sorry*, spoken in varying orders,
velaric, almost, and often, swallowed.
Each animal forms a binary system
with one of the feral chickens of Kauai.
They believe they are an island. Some are
able to camouflage as kitchen-made satellites
moving across telephone wires. They collect
open-window data, half-lives of half-heard
conversations. They party trick refuse, ingest,
then leave it on porches, neatly, in curls. Each
individual hair on their coat is an antenna
to an auxiliary. They reclaim old pelts, cold
crowns, from attics, to commune with their dead,
and wonder why we pick our brushes clean.
They believe we invented the rat and car tire.
Understand construction cranes to be a form
of prayer. They take more meaning
from the lay of flagstones than they should.
They're partial to the sound of human crying.
They sleep unmolested in the eaves
we'll never finish paying for.

SLEEP STUDY

It was the time I messaged experts. Asked after
Jake brakes, get-out plans, how the weather is written,
and what would have happened if something happened
twenty-five years ago to someone else, somewhere else.
It was a series of questions to fill the gaps
that yawned open in the small hours. The answers
later funnelled back by dutiful officiants. Emails signed
with first initials shouldered against familial names
too common to mean anything. Although, if pressed,
there might be some relation, a trace of rust in the communal
well. What we share is endurance for the mundane.
A distance runner stranded on sandy cay.
Every angle of the single palm addressed. The questions,
I offered, were for a large project, but, if requested, could not
produce a single page or formula. I asked the president
of a cartage company how they moved freight home
after, hypothetically, an accident, or what we call accidents
when conflicting intents intersect. To others:
How quickly can the border be closed if needed?
Do animals dream? How long can you live
without sleep? The marine engineer never responded
to questions about the load-bearing nature
of the international bridge. Nor the ornithologist
on a polar-blown frigate, that left as I arrived.

RED-EYE

Young uncle, barely old enough to be a father,
invites me, goddaughter, upstairs. To where
the goats were penned last year and are no longer.

For a time, the holds were filled with unwanted
furniture, boxes of what, we didn't know. A coyote
skull weighing down a hospital-grade baby scale.

Albums of brides who left twenty years ago
and cousins whose whereabouts are tabbed
with thumbnails of headstones. Things

we were done with, or they were done with us,
but we couldn't let go of like the tarped boats
of Motown summers now beached mid-avenue.

A flat, red bulb hangs above a hatch of hay,
cairns of pellets and the living fur of high holiday
church. Nailed to the wall, two tiny nooses.

I wondered whose necks were so small until
the rabbit's back feet were slipped in and cinched.
He's here to show me a trick. How life can be

turned off like a light switch if your finger is
a crowbar. Pink nebula, cosmic spray
across the barn boards. If I look down, I can see

through them like ribs. Somewhere, I read
that barns are red because stars are dying, but cannot
remember why. Here – see – the sky is dented tin.

ALMANAC

Breed an irrational hatred of hostas. Disappointment the micro-desert was greener than expected and bisected with a boardwalk, information plaques and return ticket. The newspaper shames you daily. National writ personal. When you feel guilty, google how to make your own Big Mac, your own secret sauce. Your desire droughts. Think of renting a car and travelling south. Marry the man or woman – you can't recall – on the news who spray-painted their dead lawn green. An enviable adherence to restrictions. Did I mention the thing about the hostas? Plant seeds – Pompeii tomatoes, chives and sweet basil – in dollar store dirt pucks that promise nothing but deliver. Stand ahead of the bet. In each aisle, wager where the lead is. Count the hairs in your drain. When the house cat eats the chives to the roots and pukes for days, punish the plant by putting it outside before last frost. In Britain they call hostas *plantain lilies*, but let's not get started on that. The oncoming clouds look like pulsing ellipses that disappear the promise they pixeled. Sex free-floats in heirloom categories. First scoff then click. Trust you'll know what to do in the end. Plant your focal points in pleasing patterns. Stolons firing. You're likely to get more than you put in if you time it right.

SQUALL

Treed eighteen-feet high   in a field   once thought owned,

not rented, now borrowed.   If I let go now,

what will have me?   To date, only Earth's earth,

but I'm hopeful.   We've already   taught the deer, who arrive

sudden as a squall, we can   appear from above and now

must teach ourselves. You said,   *Wrong goal. Wrong question.*

Watch your step. Don't fall   *on your way up.* You disappeared

into the treeline cast in the role   of background,   which is more

difficult than it looks. So many   working parts,   muffled sounds,

conflicting needs. To root   or be eaten.   To eat or live

the morning. It's hard to act   natural when

natures differ.   I think back to my time

on our moon, which was not   my time, but I recall it so

when I like. I dropped   a small hammer and falcon

feather, wagered   which

would strike ground first   though already knew   the answer.

I looked

out and Venn'd past and future   arrivals to find myself

left with two moons   and no home. Eventually, you

reappear with a wave that says,   *Come down, come down.*
            Your face masked,

            mouthless, otherly behind   the crystalline. Mine

        the mirror.   Trying to follow

        the path of one flake   like trying to nail your eye

to a single tree as the car   speeds past. Leaving, I ask

        if the deer will bolt on sight,

            what last chance we have left.   Your answer: it will take

                        them time to recognize us

                    as human. We lumber back
to the bulrush-stashed truck.

        With key and flare of gas,   ignite our departure.

            Dressed as nothing

        to report, dressed as no

            answer, dressed in gravity.

FLYBY

Stand at the sharp end of a shark's tooth
of beach, inch back as tidal waters dull the point.
You split the tall grass and retreat.
Downriver, a voice. *I think this is too far,*
to unseen companions. Ticks, small
as the graphite tip long buried
in your palm, constellate your legs.
Two days until Pluto. The small
have an invested interest in the small.
You are on vacation and reading
about Lyme disease. New reports
on Pluto. Daily, teenagers shore up.
Hexagons and a whale's tail.
They strip and dress driftwood
with triangles of wet Lycra. Unlit
jack-o'-lantern eyes. Yesterday, a local
asked, *Do you realize you use pronouns*
when you talk about spacecraft?
Inquire after ticks. The ounce of cremains
aboard the probe. Nine years, three billion
miles, the afterlife of Tombaugh's
ashed eye. A text to an outdated question
blinks awake. *All good. Just revelry.*
Open your computer, type *Define*
revelry. An issue with constant values
and constant invalidation of facts.
Define fact. The dwarf's dwindling
atmosphere, five natural satellites.
Etymology tick. From a window, watch
a girl swim to the closest island.

Don't *worry*, a boy yells. *Not enough salt*
for sharks. To the tick to the bird
to the girl, I whisper, Dog*fish.*
And something about love.

WHAT HE ATE DID NOT SO MUCH
RELIEVE HIS HUNGER

We're working our eyes off.
HOLGER SIERKS

The plan: ten years. The arrival precise, but with a slower landing.
The gravity lesser than where we started, turpentine sucked out

of the paint can. A negotiation of first-hand for relay, trading
one rock for another, smaller. The French president

dons his stereoscopics and we all lean back
on the collective couch. Now that the comet has us,

the industry of our concern commences its endless,
terrible orbit. The plot points predetermined, a susurrus

in the front rows, a reportage of all who've seen this
before, or something like it, a flickering of cellular

lights flickering out. Failed harpoons that cause us pause
or bounce. An aside: nights when the outlet seems too far

from bed to ignite a lean, I imagine the end of the world.
That I have the only phone left to call the only other

for which I have the number but dead battery.
Or else I'm just too tired. A switch of tools and theatre,

whichever depending on where the nostalgia hurts
less or is less current. Arguments we could have

lassoed this princely island like a country song
written by committee while the Tinkertoy pilot fish

tilts away from the sun and winds down
into failure. The view, before it goes dark until summer,

unveiled to us like the universe's oldest Polaroid. Forgotten
and found between the walls of the living house. Not yours,

but rented. The heaviest pieces of furniture abandoned
to your care because you opened the door.

All of space appears bent with no place to stand. The keel
of a shifting gaze with a black hole staked in the middle.

The eye no longer fixed or even ours, but shared. Here,
on earth, a study of children who recognize percentages

of disappointment more easily than others. Embedded training.
They spy angry wedged into the crags of everything

like love notes. Streets, doors, trees. Turn their faces
toward the sky. This filthy snowball is pissed, cringing

and waiting for the perihelion spin to reveal itself
more fully. Or maybe it's a chip of ice spinning,

space-born berg that will one day melt itself out
of our stare, or the reverse. Until then, a dust Rorschach

where every answer is breasts or home. Between
the morning's forecast and messages on how

to keep the rats out, the radio transmits the hum
of our most far-flung worry, calls it *song*.

ARC

Movement so fast it ceases to be seen.
You'd call it art if it could be framed right.
Given the right conditions, you, too, could
fly. Or a wing through the gut of the fuselage
could make quick mince of best plans. A
thousand would-be breaths shorn. A dead-
heading of airbag subflora. Pinned to the
tarmac, wait to be launched into moderate
space. Something you can return from, only
more tired from having made the intimate
acquaintance of strangers, their stray habits
and habitats. Taking the elevator up to the
floor above the one you live on might as
well be sky. It's not like you'll go back. It's
not like you'll call. Everything we need to
leave leaves on blade or axle. Princess-box-
spin without the tinkle of song that springs
up on fused legs and says secure your seat
belt and know your exits. The destination
is Ersilia's cat's cradle or Thekla's cranes.
It will be decided upon landing. Tell me
you've heard this one before, a passenger
counts his fingers before he gives up and
starts again. Another recounts a Dallas
convention for high-end bathroom fixtures.
Like, really high end. Gas is channelled
through the walls to keep us airborne and
warm. A seatmate's whiskey-Ativan slur
lullabies an ascent you're sure you've made
before. Slow to reveal the edges, Saturn's
cold rings spin us low. The brain a hard-
wired bedtime story of statistics on what
mistake might be greater than this. Trying
to carry a shotgun over a fence? Living
alone and slipping on a tongue of soap?
Thinking the gap in traffic is passable? Look
down, the world collects its gold in grids.

VIRGA

One sister city leans into the other, communiqué
threaded above an inward cat's cradle

of CCTV. Secrets make them feel they have more
to offer one another

even if artificially united like bad taxidermy or a week
of leftovers. A steady

funnel of tourists on varying orbits revisit monuments
to good intentions

and their failures. *Father drowned trying to save son,
drowned.* It's telling

that either way you travel it, arrival is familiar.
Milk in bags or cartons.

Roofs flat or peaked. Breasts held up by cloth or let go.
One city's sun appears

white while the other dawns the lamp-opposing side
of an empty eggshell. Unviable

for the long term, but no need to bring that up just yet.
Cities where once every twenty years

they exchange their best livestock, jams and machinery.
Let's be honest: second best.

One hangs bunting. One wears it. Each city
an early warning system

for the other without the ability to access the
particulars. Water-filled bunkers

that walleye the view of the contents and what went
wrong. And it all went wrong

a while ago, but no one's telling. Both weathermen
predict a mild winter,

but not which one wants it, which does not. Each will
purposefully leave a shed unlocked

to see what goes missing. Yet, come morning,
unable to recall everything they've lost.

SYMPATHETIC STRINGS

A lake with its many shacks. Discernible
by their colours, size and lack of personal

adornment. We know which is ours
by which are not. Yearly expansions

and retractions. Corrections made
under duress of seasons, bad

dreams, and superstition. We've baited
the water with everything the water

already has. Our trick is no trick, but time
and halo of attention. We owed ourselves

that much. One thing that was easy.
Below, fish strung like bunting

ring topside brass. Dinner bells.
In twenty years, it will become clear

the child within the frame of attention
will look like her father's mother

and act like her father's father. A leap
of manner and pathology. Jumping a ditch

and clearing a small, undiscovered sun.
We thread monofilament through the ice.

Frozen Nipissing a badly sewn button attached
to more crudely made us. And yet, these bodies

resonate. Dampen one and a second starts the same
conversation, only now, theirs.

Here, as we wait, listen: the wind threaded
through another winter's wrecked shack.

THIS IS GRAVITY

said a man on the radio as a twist of the dial
shifted the thought into the past.
From the train, you see wind turbines bend
down to shred the corn. They say, *You were gone*
too long. Look what you made us do.
Sleeping among strangers is like watching
a low-burning brush fire with first loves.
The turn of their mouths obscured by failures
of lighting and destination. On return,
there will be another chance at a chance.
There are only so many faces to go around.
Home is where the heave is. Where the harbour is.
Where hotel. We buried our dogs in plots
of earth the owner finally cut us off from.
Through the door of the car that collects you,
call them. *Here, boys. Come, brothers.* And wait
for the fields to rattle with their love coming home.

MOTHER, ORDER APPLE

The radio reports there are no
apples this year, so you drive

to the closest orchard and ask
for apples. *I would like to buy apples.*

When the man at the chained gate
tells you there are none, you say:

I want apples. You tell him
there have always been apples.

Fifty-seven years of apples.
He tells you to drive west

two thousand miles. You'll find apples
there, just down the road

from here. He says if you'd died
in surgery as expected, you would

not be without apples this year.
A perfect record.

Maybe he didn't say those words
exactly, but you knew

he was thinking them
as he walked away to where he keeps

shelves of canned halves, the ones
he saved for a year like this.

FINAL REPORT ON THE STATUS OF
RACCOONS ON FERN AVENUE

The black walnut tree tosses its fruit
onto garage roofs, already heavy
eaves, dots i's all down the alley
where one summer we watched
a peacock, escaped, launch from roof
to roof. Contracts have been made
with several futures. One future,
yours, regrets its small, clawed hands.
Its limited reach but perfect recall.
Its compulsion to wash things
before devouring them. Its ability
to see you without you seeing it.

Once, upstreet, I fought through crowds
to better see a person who looked
like someone I loved, you, but twenty
years older. With an apology
on how black walnut can poison
a plot, a horse, but salvage the meat
of a heart, I excused myself. My life,
like the peafowl, went on for several blocks.

Overhead, an Aero L-39 Albatros
is pollinating the black-eyed Susans
and forgetting the flowers butterflies
are partial to because it is partial to others.
Late summer's gutted warplanes
drop a spectacle of contrails, reverse
engineer crowds into singles stationed
in front of newscasts on Sunday evenings.

Outside, there are four overripe tomatoes
left on the stunted tomato plant.
I imagine one of them is the moon, hung
soft beside a lamppost confusing
the view, de Montaigne's sleeping face,
or a plane at the bottom of our ability
to dredge a memory. It helps.

Your boxes, potted plants are gathered
next to the eye of the kitchen window
that oversaw the weeds double annually,
give cover to the rats who only wanted
the company of your ancient cat –
at times blind – and left, interstellar,
with him. It was never about you.

This is the truth of the years as I recall it.
So should you. The black box
was only ever a black box. If I hum
the "Song of the Volga Boatmen,"
will the raccoons who can no longer perch
on the ledge of your sleep be soothed?

ANOTHER EARTH

Pound for pound, our love is driven into ditches.
The call and response of ten-codes, like a teenager's
exacting will. When there's too much to say, say less.

The conversation since turned monologue to the cinerary
urn repurposed as one man's last stand. The constant worry
if a speck of you was smuggled into the mix of his.
A grain of flour undetected in the eternal contraband.

Walking home, the streetside dead rabbit of morning
is the same streetside dead rabbit of evening, now hardened.
A petrification of mislocation and thoughts of what you would do
knee-deep in the county where you once held the hearts
of small things in your hands, thumbed the livery flesh
like a beat or a lesson for a problem years in the making.
An age when it was easy to mistake a full stomach
for a heart. Or death as something to fill you.

Never good at confrontation, you once stood in a tower
taller than your best arguments. Lied and said you loved
brutalism until you learned it meant concrete and not cruel.

Tonight, let something else take the strikes.
Below the streets, chapped rails spark, beg a reading.
Turn transit transfers over like tarot. It will always be
what you were hoping for, just not how you wanted it.
An empty apartment when all you needed was a bus ticket.
A stranger's one-sided fight climbing rented pipes
as you washed the number you could call off your palm.

Accusations of avoidance are accurate. But
like Hernandez's lilies, you busy yourself, infinitely
puke your milk into the river. Overhead, a helicopter.
white for traffic, orange for emergency. Or maybe
a search for someone lost or running – a long finger
of light detangling ravines of their canted dark.

You indulge the small, terrible part of your mind that hopes
for an escape. An alternate theory as of yet unproven.
The man of your news-at-six imagination stands
outside your door with an alternate universe in his hands.
A single loosed earring reveals the entire equation. The tail slate
claps shut. Then the flip of the channel to find you alive
on a set that's supposed to be Nebraska or Minnesota.
There is a heartening misunderstanding with a neighbour.
No one wears patterns. The cans say only *peas*, only *carrots*.
A fence demarcates what's yours as long as you can hold on to it.
You want it to be that easy. To cuckoo into a new life –
to place your fork in a drawer of forks, and let it go unnoticed.

The helicopter nears. Tonight, even the air is filled with bodies.
And in your pocket, a key to a motorbike you abandoned
on an island in the South China Sea sixteen years ago,
although you can no longer recall where you last left it,
or with whom. This key that will not unlock the next door.

MOTE

The husk of a housefly bowled
into the kitchen light like something
in your eye that would cause more harm
than good to remove. Instead,
live with it. Look around it. The lamp
a dish thrown and arrested mid-air.
Suspended by something like regret,
but not quite. Wishing you'd been born
a twin or an owl. Yet, the light is still
mostly light and the singular shadow
invisible under the compound
cloud that cast it. Mostly

you only look up when someone visits.
And when you do, the cloud is fly-
shaped. Your visitors, you assume, note
what you have not removed, invent
excusable excuses. The chair
with its hidden rot. The dark or height
you'd rather not stand in. Later,
alone, you see the fly, years dead,
as a small, wrecked plane
on your smaller island. It's a matter
of relativity. You'd call it a blind spot
if it wasn't the only thing you can see.

SHIFT OF OCCUPANT

I prospect the 765th return to the second
floor of the same bay-and-gable. The house
still standing in the middle of its ovate
ring of efficient hostas. Perennial, invasive,
the house risen atop traditional land taken
for coffee shops, stores of convenience,
pizzerias. We buried the rivers before they
could cross us. The holy glow of the 7-Eleven
where I fetch the morning milk. The place
I am least afraid, standing in its overlit
aisles, because it never closes and the milk
is always cold. I live under the insistent care
and cover of realtor cards that invite the
landlord to sell. Across the street, children
bat a star of shuttlecock between them. No
net. Just me, in periphery, digging into the
mailbox again for algorithms the object
cannot draft or contain. At the height of
future anonymous, the girls may one day
recall me, but not know why. What preferred
memory, necessary number, equation
sacrificed because of the way repetition
gets stuck in the jaw of the brain? Behind
the alley behind my house, a building. And
behind it, a second, taller. On top, a backlit
human who stands, sometimes sits, and
other times catalogues the latest terrestrial
sunset. Sundown, sun-up for an entire life
even though your finger has been on the
switch. A field of yellow rapeseed flowers.

Fridge full of uniform plastic jugs of mixed milk. Octopus DNA slipped into the sea when we were too young a species or not present to understand potential outcomes. I cannot recall why my eyes are hazel or why I wear my blood on the inside. Tell me, have I become scared of the dark or simply frightened of places not wired for light? I know I promised I would stop talking about space, even though we're staked in the middle of our view of it, stranded on a rift of raft moving at the pace human fingernails grow. My own chewed to the quick to arrest yet another lateral move. Born to degrade, I figure going down is the only way up.

PARALLAX

At the assumed midpoint, you open
a book, dart a finger to a sentence.

Take note of who and what's at play. Draw lines
as the train draws its own. Ouija a future

ghost through the errands of a future day, which,
today is only one: Point A to Point Almost-

B. You could bet lunch on what's coming
on the lunches you've had.

The teenager across the aisle is making
her own notes. She hides her pink-and-white journal

with a carefully angled elbow. Eating a best-before
July 6 sandwich, she already knows everyone

imagines themselves onto her page. Even poorly
or in passing. You both saw the red fox

streak across the field between the last
two towns. She, like you, is the false centre,

but like Mauna Kea, the best vantage availed.
Near the end, you'll talk. Wager guesses

at one another's ages, each off by years
in opposing directions. *I don't have children*

is the excuse you offer. She, recently a child,
offers none. Her error, at some point before her birth,

correct. She can't guess how far you've gone
and will not return from. Yours was, at best,

a best guess. Fortune-telling. Or a stone tossed
at the closest moon to turn out the sun's recurring light.

LAST DAYS

The trick to hurtling through space or sea
in the emptied gas can that may double

as your coffin is extra doors. Amputate
what's flooded with prehistoric hunger,

or shuck the extra weight on order
while there's still someone to command.

It's better to act before you can think
consequence. A slight of hand where

you're both on stage and in the audience.
Decompression will always take two minutes

longer than you have. Mating will keep
you alive. Find someone to bunk down with

in tight corners. It's not an orgasm,
it's the entire human race at stake. So come

surface or terraform, you'll harbour
an indifferent curl of cells that will learn

your language only to say you're not
the world. Here, the floors are tiled

with convenience: hidden caverns unhidden
by the man you knew from the get-go would

push the don't-push button. Your persistent use
of light. Your persistent interest in the light

below the second moon's ice. Just one more
look. Communications are out.

How you're always losing things, even
yourself, which you find in the gut

of an unrecorded Russian scuttle. Three days
of a six-month mission left. The directive

must be completed. It's why you're here. It was
a one-way ticket. You knew that from the start.

CONTACT

Cloud cover like a badly made bed, ruched in sections, rushed.
Whatevered for reasons of a lifetime of do overs. Why bother
trying to change? The gathered duvet sometimes mimics you,
makes double. Dopples a decoy. An escape plan. The safety
of numbers and cover. When the wing dips, a hole in the sky
revealed. Until then, a man in the aisle seat. Calculations
to see if it's possible to slide through the fish-eye window
if he touches your thigh again, your face. We like our planes
fashioned after ships. The illusion one could jump or be forced
off and possibly survive between the distance and everything
that wants to live how it's always lived. Without compromise.
When does knowing a person begin? Was it when he noted
you look like his ex-wife? Hair naturally red, not like yours. Fake.
He can tell, but it's okay. What your children together would look like.
That if you had been born in Fayetteville, he would've liked
to have known you. Feels he does. Not like the absent husband
his mind weds you to. The one who abandoned you to his company
like a firing squad to its post waiting for a reason to prove worth.
The moment he asked for vodka on the fifty-three-minute flight
from Charlotte to Wilmington to bridge the gap between
pre- and post-flight beers. Or how he lifted his shirt to show you
where his lungs had been punctured and once collapsed,
he said he'd briefly died and now is, briefly, alive.

TRANSIT OF MERCURY

The freckle on my sister's hazel iris replicates
the May transit of Mercury across our sun.

Every thirteen or thirty-three years, orbits line up to make theory
believable to the layman splayed out on Earth

like a poor man's star made of lesser dust.
For a span of hours she becomes a universe.

And yet, I have no sister. She would have smoked
and blown blue out windows, into exhaust vents.

Our DNA flickering like ancient Christmas lights
that eventually burn down the house. Her hand,

the one I held before somersaulting back into a black pool
of anaesthetic, waking corrected into her security.

Or the night our father left, and I held hers. Pressed
into life like a fiver for a favour to be called in

later, at forty-two my sister taught me to drive.
I leaned over and held the still-warm wheel

while she put up her hands as if surrendering
to greater authority. Only ever heir to her

absence, I tried to sister my mother, another's sister,
a stranger, a man, air. So when I say I miss you,

it's not to you, but through to the palm trees
on the throw pillow that are not actual palms.

But I enjoy the idea of their shade
when the sun hits them right.

NOTES

"I Come Around with Appetite to Parties": The title is a line from Eileen Myles' poem "keats & I" from Not Me (Semiotext(e), 1991).

"You Wore Out Your Welcome with Radiant Ability": The title is a variation on a lyric from Pink Floyd's "Shine On You Crazy Diamond."

"Prototype": The "holy measure" is a reference to the international prototype of the kilogram (IPK), which is stored in a vault at the International Bureau of Weights and Measures in Parc de Saint-Cloud, Sèvres, France.

"Listen Before Transmit": This poem was inspired by and riffs off of Peter Gizzi's poem "Pretty Sweety."

"Pioneer 14": "A separate recording will play" refers to the Voyager Golden Records. "Linda" is Linda Salzman Sagan. While Carl Sagan and Frank Drake designed the plaques for the Pioneer space probe, Salzman Sagan, an artist, prepared the artwork. As a condition of approval, NASA required the pudendal cleft be removed from the image of the woman. Note: the man's penis remained. Only two genders were depicted in the plaque.

"Report on the Bright Spots on Ceres": NASA launched the Dawn space probe in September 2007.

"Watched by the Drone": Is a cento. Each line is from, with permission, one side of a years-long email conversation.

"The Omega Trick": Is after Matt Bahen's painting The Judge. The epigraph is from Kate Hall's poem "Overnight a Horse Appeared" from The Certainty Dream (Coach House Books, 2009).

"Memoir": Is for Kate McQuaid.

"A Brief History": The epigraph is a line from *Les Navigateurs de l'infini* by J-H Rosny aîné (Joseph Henri Honoré Boex). The book includes the first instance of the word *astronaut* – "astronautique."

"Minus Time": Is titled after the novel *Minus Time* by Catherine Bush.

"Report on the Status of Raccoons on Fern Avenue": The final line is borrowed from the *Globe and Mail* article "In Toronto's War on 'Raccoon Nation,' I'm Siding with the Critters" by Elizabeth Renzetti.

"Flyby": References the New Horizons space probe. Clyde Tombaugh was the astronomer who discovered Pluto in 1930. A small amount of his ashes was placed aboard the probe.

"What He Ate Did Not So Much Relieve His Hunger": The title is a line from *Moby-Dick* by Herman Melville. Holger Sierks was the principal investigator of OSIRIS, the imaging system on the orbiter of ESA's Rosetta mission to Comet 67P/ Churyumov-Gerasimenko. The quote is from the *Globe and Mail* article "Philae's First Comet Photos Include Ominous Signs of Probe's Fate" by Ivan Semeniuk. The final line – "the radio transmits the hum of our most far-flung worry, calls it song" – is a reference to the comet's "song" as captured by the Rosetta spacecraft.

"Arc": Is for Emily Keeler. Ersilia and Thekla are cities in Italo Calvino's book *Invisible Cities*.

"Another Earth": Is titled after the film *Another Earth* written by Mike Cahill and Brit Marling.

"But / like Hernandez's lilies, you busy yourself, infinitely / puke your milk into the river" is an adaptation of "Calla lily is doubled-over by a riverbank / puking milk" from "Comment Thread in Response to '100 Best Flowers of the Year'" by David Hernandez.

"Parallax": Mauna Kea, a dormant volcano, is home to Mauna Kea Observatories (MKO), one of the best places on our world to look up and out.

ACKNOWLEDGEMENTS

Earlier versions of some of the poems in this book were first published, sometimes with different titles, in the following publications. Thank you to the editors and staff of each publication.

Ambit (UK): "This is Gravity," "Arc," and "Virga"

The Awl (US): "I Come Around With Appetite to Parties" and "What He Ate Did Not So Much Relieve His Hunger"

Arc: "Pioneer 14"

Best Canadian Poetry in English 2016: "Black Sea Nettle"

Boston Review (US): "You Wore Out Your Welcome With Radiant Ability"

The Dark Horse (UK): "Mother, Order Octopoda"

The Fiddlehead: "Another Earth"

Forget Magazine: "Watched by the Drone"

Grain: "Red-eye" and "Clonal"

The Malahat Review: "A Casual Defence" and "The Omega Trick"

NewPoetry: "Prototype"

Plenitude Magazine: "A Brief History"

Poetry (US): "Contact"

PRISM international: "Black Sea Nettle"

The Puritan: "Transit of Mercury" and "Mote"

The Rusty Toque: "Report on the Bright Spots on Ceres" and "Flyby"

Taddle Creek: "Report on the Status of Raccoons on Fern Avenue"

The Windsor Review: "Small Orange and Blue," "Forecast," "Or In Argument," "Minus Time," Sleep Study," "Shift of Occupant," "Parallax," and "Last Days"

Thank you:

To the Ontario Arts Council and the Canada Council for the Arts for the generous funding that allowed me the time to work on the book.

To the National Water Centre, located outside Saint John, New Brunswick. For the important work you do, space to write and introduction to the Kennebecasis River, which, upon diving into, I found was much, much colder than expected. To only learning about dogfish after the jump.

To Jim Johnstone for editing and publishing the chapbook *Black Sea Nettle* (Anstruther Press). To Erica Smith for making it beautiful.

To Noelle Allen, Ashley Hisson, and everyone at Buckrider Books and Wolsak & Wynn for all that you do. Your dedication to poetry, to poets. To Natalie Olsen for inspired and gorgeous design and layout. I am deeply indebted to my editor Paul Vermeersch for considering every angle. You made this book better. I'm grateful.

To Grace O'Connell, Tracy Pumfrey, Daniel Scott Tysdal, Jennifer LoveGrove, Stefanie Stevanovich, David Leonard, Teva Harrison, Zoe Whittall, Bianca Spence, David James Brock, and so many others. For conversation and kaleidoscopic knowledge.

To the countless writers, poets, photographers, directors, actors, musicians, composers, painters, researchers, journalists, scientists, mathematicians, engineers, far-flung spacecraft and landers, and Earthly flora and fauna that sparked exploration, imagination, and reimagination.

To Carolyn Black for always making me reconsider what language can do.

To David Seymour, with love, for so much. Your poems, intelligence, and care. Low wave. Pillar lean.

To my family, especially my parents, Réal and Debbie Couture, who are the stars pinned above any and every road I travel down. To my grandparents Kathy and Vic Deneau for being beacons on the edge of Lake Erie. To my beautiful Aunt Laurie. To Liette Couture and Richard Trudeau for our time at Lac des Sittelles and Lac Memphrémagog. To my grandmother Simone Bélanger for all the little secrets you ask me to keep.

To Jos. Couture. Who we miss but see echoes of in every good thing.

DANI COUTURE is the author of several collections of poetry and the novel Algoma (Invisible Publishing). From 2012 to 2016, she was the Poetry and Fiction Editor at This Magazine. Couture's work has been nominated for the Trillium Book Award for Poetry, received an honour of distinction from the Writers' Trust of Canada's Dayne Ogilvie Prize for Emerging LGBTQ Writers, and won the ReLit Award for Poetry. Her poems have appeared in publications in Canada, the US, and the UK, and several editions of Best Canadian Poetry in English.